When I Drowned

When I Drowned

Poems by

Lauren Davis

Cover design by Shay Culligan
Cover image by Ahmad Odeh via Unsplash

ISBN: 978-1-63980-201-2

Kelsay Books
502 South 1040 East, A-119
American Fork, Utah 84003
Kelsaybooks.com

for Charlie, always

Acknowledgments

2River: "Father Fills the Tanks with Bleach," "Floyd Spreads Famine on His Black Horse"

Anti-Heroin Chic: "Two Decades after the Flood the Doctors Still Don't Know What Is Wrong with My Brother's Body"

Deep South Magazine: "My God, My Government," "Cope, Children"

Poetry South: "If I Drink It," "Five Hundred Eighty Miles Floyd Stretches His Arms," "Emzara Says," "My Good Christ"

The Swamp: "Quitting the Home, September 1999"

The section "The Missing Ones" was published as a limited-edition chapbook by Winter Texts.

I owe limitless gratitude to the writers, family, and friends who have helped support me and my work throughout the years.

Karen Kelsay, Delisa Hargrove, Peter Davies, Julie Kelsay, Abbie Davies, Jenna Sumpter, and Shay Culligan for giving this book shape and life. Conner Bouchard-Roberts, for your care and support of the Lake Crescent poems. Eric Muhr, who brought my debut full-length *Home Beneath the Church* into being. Jan Bailey and George Singleton, who first helped me find my voice. Thank you, always, to the South Carolina Governor's School for the Arts and Humanities. Mark Wunderlich, Timothy Liu, David Daniel, April Bernard, and Major Jackson, who made my years at Bennington a profound journey. The Writers' Workshoppe, where the poets go to blossom. Risa Denenberg, Jayne Marek, Kelli Russell Agodon, and Ronda Broatch—the exquisite Upstairs Poets. Lauren Brazeal, whose close reading of this manuscript helped birth its final form. Samantha Ladwig and Thom. The writers Elijah Burrell, Sandra Yannone, Jennifer Porter, Maura Snell, Pam Dionne, Judy Borenin, Joanne Clarkson, Laura Schaeffer, Denton Loving, Elaine Fletcher Chapman, Gary Lemons, Michael Schmeltzer, Kathryn Hunt, Gary Copeland Lilley—the world is a better place because of your poetry, prose, and art. Meaghan Quinn, my sister poet, thank you for your honesty, your friendship, your enduring support.

Justin, who treaded through the waters.

The missing ones, and those who love you.

The community of Rocky Mount, North Carolina. When the storm came, you came together.

Enheduanna, and all your Gods and Goddesses.

Forever my love, Charlie. For this life, and the next, and the next, and the next. I am yours, all of me.

Contents

Tar River, Rise

The Missing Ones

On July 3, 1929, Russell Warren picked up his wife, Blanch, from the hospital. He bought a new washing machine and paid the grocery bill. They drove U.S. Route 101 along Lake Crescent towards their home in Port Angeles, Washington. They'd promised to celebrate the Fourth of July with their sons. But the couple did not arrive home. The two boys never saw their parents again.

Blanch Speaks

There are dangers
in deep waters kept

silent. Like dark
that climbs the spine.

There's a stain on the rock
unfolding. I drink the lake,

all of it. I make it mine.

Seven Thousand Years Ago

Lake Crescent was a raven flying.
    The shoreline overwatered.
Fish rainbowed within their native range.

The earthquake cut a drowned country
    for us to rest.
In these depths, God laid out a marriage bed.

We Died on a Wednesday

Though we'd promised the boys we'd take them
to Sol Duc to celebrate the Fourth of July. My husband left

them a pocket watch and $35 in case of emergencies
before he came to fetch me, which is to say,

he must have had a premonition. We never returned.
Our sons heard the rumors we've abandoned them.

Decades later, Frank will perish when his body swells—
edema, and fluid in his lungs. Charles will disappear

in the ocean. We shall become a family with nothing
but mouths full of water.

Remember Our Wedding

I wore white, a belt with a rectangular buckle
larger than my hand. You combed your hair

straight down the middle. As lovely as a solider
before his first battle. Your sister also married

that day, which meant more peonies.
They named me—*Worthy young lady.*

Inside my belly, our first child kicked.
When I did not drink wine, you did not drink wine.

Things That Are Pleasing

Warm temperatures that settle beneath moonlight.
Pine needles in my hair.
The sounds of small children on the shore.
Beardslee trout dancing.
A rainstorm I hear but cannot feel.
The smell of winter in hidden splits.
My husband's eyes in the depths.

I'll Tell You What Happened

I'd been dreaming. Russell fell asleep, too. So when the curve
in the road came the car drifted into the lake. Branches near
the shore snapped. Otherwise, night watched without a sound.

He'd done it before, nodded off on this highway,
but not so fatally. Ten miles per hour we traveled
to our gravesite. He never even braked.

I awoke with the lake against my door.
We fell far into the depth's mouth
before kicking out of the tin trap.

This is how it feels to drown:
You'll try not to inhale, but you will.
Because the brain wants what it wants.

Water will fill the lungs. When your beloved drifts by
you will be unable to reach your hands to him.
Just try to move a single muscle. Your eyes will

stay open. Your husband has something to tell you—
you can sense it in the cold. Wait until you are both done
drowning. Then build a new home.

Elegant Things

Sapphire water midday.
A hint of elk antlers on the water's skin.
Sounds of an eagle crying.
An owl feather refusing to sink.
Fishing line snaking slowly past my pillow.
My husband's lips while he sleeps.

What Makes the Lake So Thirsty

We are not the only mislaid ones.
They rest at separate depths.
My husband makes the women blush,
the men slap their knees.

We are the republic of secrets
and missing person cases. I was thirty-three.
I wore my least favorite dress to our death.
The lake floor is a reversed sky,

a dozen wedding rings glinting like satellites.
Tell me the lake has needs. Tell me the lake
is full of greed. I'll believe you. The water deceives—
calm and quiet as a beast overwintering.

Have You Seen My Boys?

They are absent from my arms.
Voices never call *Mother*.
I know their bodies

will change despite me.
Beard stubble, rich muscle,
and no one to tell them the truth.

My love haunts good
as any ghost. It is more
than lake deep. Boys—

I am never so buried,
hemorrhaged with blue
that I forget you.

At the body of the lake
I lie with my jaw open,
chanting your names.

Things That Irritate

Clatter of traffic on Sundays.
The sharp words of a couple bickering on any day.
Candy wrappers floating into my bedroom.
Friends who never visit.
Long weeks without rain.
Divers that swim past my outstretched fingers.

When the Lady of the Lake Comes to Stay

"The woman's face was unrecognizable, but her body had not decomposed."
—Mavis Amudson, *The Lady of the Lake*

Russell, we have a visitor
and nothing to offer—
no cake, no coffee.

Let us share our home
with its many rooms of water.

Empty the bed of trout for Hallie to lay her head.
Witness her drift down towards us

in her tattered burial gown, her face
losing features. But look how
pure her skin beneath each bruise.

May she forgive our lack
of hospitality, our lack of cutlery.

Husband, welcome her.
Do not leave her out in the cold.

We will give up our privacy, wholly,
perhaps. She'll share our nightly communion
with distant owls and all our others.

Rare Things

Weeks without a boat on our backs.
Light on your eyelashes.
Disagreements over what we name each fish.
Minutes that I do not miss our sons.
Green herons.
Decades without new bodies.
Sounds of laughter in predawn air.

The Silver Snake Pin

It glints with twelve small jewels. Where the thirteenth
had gone missing, I placed a scrap of tinfoil.

Do you know what happens when you lift serpents
from depths where they've adapted to the bitter and black?

Divers find the pin secured to an unfinished blouse,
the one that floated from my lap the night I died.

I've spent years listening to the snake's stories.
It belongs away from the living. Refuse to look it

in the eyes. After shedding its first skin—
you will see its stuttered silence misleads.

The Lady of the Lake Leaves

Hallie learns to float, a magic trick.
Hogtied and strangled, weighted.

Though this new day
does not deny her.

Transformed into wax.
Her purity would make even Christ weep.

My husband sings as she rises.
It's an old hymn about snow.

She is a vision or deity.
How many detectives must touch her body?

"1940, afternoon of July 6—"

Lake Crescent for the first time returns
one of its dead. The first and only time.

Louise Rolf in a fishing skiff spotted
an oblong object. A pure white shoulder
showing through a tear in the blanket.

Down there for three years. Rope around
the ankle. Elastic garter on one leg.

Fragments of a green dress. Not a speck
of rot. A clean smell coming off her.
They put her in a potter's grave.

Hallie's husband served nine years.
But there's the matter of the lake allowing

her return. When someone drowns,
their corpse is never found. Never.
The lake doesn't take offerings. Only lives.

"It's a damn strange lake."

I was walking on the bottom.
Six hundred feet down.
Light on my feet.
I didn't feel wet or cold or anything.
Near some of the skeletons,
came a body standing straight.
A tall woman wrapped in a blanket.
I woke, the sun warming my face.

Permit Me to Clear My Throat

Below the lake—sleek as an open thigh—
I am of the body and of the body of this lake
and of the body of this half-dressed night.

The things he does with silence—
Russell, he eats it. There is not enough.

The stars are whiskey-bleached.
The moon swallows everything I tell it.
My nails are on Russell's back.

Watched by his hands.
Known by his song.

When They Find the Evidence of Us

Our sons will already be lost
to their own drownings. Divers will pull

metal and bone from Lake Crescent.
But my body will stay secret.

The things we drowned with.
Unanswered prayers.

Bread, cheese, red berries.
Each other, growing colder.

Rain in my fists. Our boys' names
in your throat. A black flower vase.

Elsewhere, ravens nest their young.

Grief Keeps

All that goes unseen—
sand shifts on that other coast.

Skyscrapers are built. Skyscrapers burn.
I missed the war.

I learn of these things from strangers
who dip their toes in our home.

They'll never know how I overhear.
How much I resent.

Was it a lived life if I did not drink
from the other lakes of legend—

if I missed my chance for flight,
to see each cloud's secret face?

In my time, I only heard one language.
Now I learn the language of none.

Hope

It has eaten each day. Rain hits
the surface of the lake and the lake
grows. The sun burns,

water dissipates.

I am not the only one,
but I am Russell's faithful bride.
My boys' true mother.

Hope eats

clean my bones. I belong
to water. Stained white,
I am the forever wife.

The Secret They Won't Tell You

Years of water, and my husband's eyes
glow blue. Lapis—steeped. Not the same face

I married. I desire him, and differently.
My fingers seek him in our always dark.

People will tell you the lake lacks nitrogen,
makes it blush sapphire. But people say

a lot of things. Come closer.
The true secret will be a soft touch.

Enheduanna's Daughter

". . . [Enheduanna] is recognized as the first author of record, the first individual known to have created a body of her own writing. . . ."

—Betty De Shong Meador, *Princess, Priestess, Poet: The Sumerian Temple Hymns of Enheduanna*

High Priestess of the Moon God of the City of Ur

Or mother—as I prefer to call you. Tonight
was the Cold Moon, ending the year.

I made a fire, though I was warm
and without need. I built this house

on the mountain green. Your picture
by my bedside—he does not know who you are.

He asks, and I answer, *History*. I answer,
All Rivers, Storm-Shot, Queenship of the Ruins.

I could call you what you are if you'd come
down and tell me, if you kept company

with something other than the gods. If I said to him
you were mother, he wouldn't hear me.

He would assume I had a bat in my throat.
He'd rush me to the nurses, and there I'd say,

Bring me mother, and they'd say,
This woman has a bat in her throat.

Your name must be close to something
like their wings, thrumming in the watery dark.

I've gone out at night and the black things find me.
They come and dress me in grey and lapis blue.

Even my wrists resemble two bruises. Watch and I'll make
a physician of myself. I'll heal my wounds with gauze

and incantations. What do I tell him? Do I keep you
secret, as if you are meant to be kept?

Mother, I Have Stolen Your Tongue

This split dark,
built for a pure, clean chamber.

Holy one—
Blood Maker.

They wrapped you
in terror and awe—

whose pure, sweet waters
shape you.

Forged in plenty,
in fire-red glow.

Heaven's ancient verdicts,
where the river lets

the true live,
but binds the dark.

You eat your heart
like a snake.

Do not enter
the house of Silence.

        She speaks—
        heaven shakes.

Come Chaste, Come Strange

Your name, illicit.
Ghost story, and in the twilight

they regret your hands.
Bride, refused. They buried you

behind the crescent white.
When I, the always daughter, sing of you,

their eyes roll back like guilt.
Enheduanna, mother, ever elegy—

bend the stone once more
and startle the sun.

Mother

My body disappears in salt-sand
seeking the bone and teeth of you.

I cannot fail. To unearth you—
my devotion. They say

your womb never kept a child.
You and I know differently.

There is one more way to give birth—
I'll never speak of it. And now

your tongue a dead thing.
But I have your last

poem. I will keep wringing
the ground for your grave.

Without you
I am unnamed.

Mother

Tell me of holy.
My body split,
while you were
kept for the gods.

Never to echo
what it is to be you—
princess, priestess,
mine. Would you believe

it, mother, if I told you
I found someone to love?
He cuts open the pear, feeds
me all. I take even the pips

of it. You were meant
to know him—his name
in your fine mouth.
At the temple how did you

hold your palms
to the heat of one sun?

Mother

I.

The soil is too dry
to sleep in. Something rumbles

in the foreground
of our home. Never tell

another, Mother—I drank

every river
that's been named.

II.

After even my seventh bath,
I feel marked.

Night will not cleanse
his hands off me.

It is good
to be unclean.

Saltwater Sleeps

I was born this morning inside the reeds.
In the cup of my hands, two doves trembling.

Alone, that is what they call me.
It's the sun I touched, and it wants me.

The lake in my mouth is suspect,
glimmering red till dusk.

I Walk to You

With whatever flowers grow
beneath trick evergreens.

       A blackbird masks her wings
       in my clutched bouquet.

It takes her only a moment
to wholly fade, but that moment—

       the pause,
       her body trembling.

Like a trap,
the moon rises

       lunatic and blank,
       hoarding your face.

My Mother Lily

Your perfume rattles
the night. In all your unfurled
tongues—a question.

       Full—the sleeping stone.
       Full—the talking sheets.

If you asked me, I would tell.
I am afraid of you. Fog spills
the moon into your mouth—

       back from history, dressed for
       a bridal shower. Reveal to me one
       more language. Stained cloud.

I am different now
from when I first came
thirsty out of the forest.

       In my hair unsung the fog.
       Lichen-covered.

Mother, desert-mind,
each sun that rose,

       rose for you. Even the moon.
       From your breasts you have fed

the city. Though remember me,
your daughter.

In my room the rain gathers.
The thunder buckles your ghost.

If I call you,
I will drown.

One time, you killed me. A hook
in my lip, and my legs were scaled.
You ate even the thin bones.

Inside your belly I grew a fish's tail.
Horizon-inked, my lips were prayers.

Tar River, Rise

"Many people were awakened by strange sounds only to discover that their homes were flooding and that the water was already too deep to leave or would be soon if they did not leave immediately."

—Alice Thorp, *Flood: Reflections of Hurricane Floyd*

Quitting the Home, September 1999

Our bags still packed from Bible Camp.
Hair still flushed with bonfire smoke.

Mother wakes us. We drive
through a newborn river
at our driveway's bottom dip.

The sky falls, defiant. We find
a public school's makeshift shelter
where strangers share our sleep.

If I am quiet here, I can catch
whispers. Someone is saying
all will be okay.

Or not. It is hard to make the words
out over the sound of rain.

Five Hundred Eighty Miles Floyd Stretches His Arms

Some do not know until he creeps
into their homes. He cracks the dark,

splits each sleeper's dream.
No boat. No ark. No bridge to yesterday.

Across townships, cement fields,
subdivisions he stitches his name. Hurls

children into drainage pipes.
Submerges bodies in cars. All our lands

glutted. Mother, father, have you
ever seen so much water?

The Fern Knew

God did us all a favor
taking back the land.

The fern knew when the sky would fall.
Each of her fronds untucked

for the soft death approaching.
A firefly crawled below
her leaves, taking measured breaths.

And Mother built her
bedchamber facing west.

To list her sins against me
would be so boring.

Our house unable to cure us
of ourselves—rooms designed
for comfort, light—sufficient.

If I Drink It

I am the flood.
Almighty. Swallowing
the village.
Devouring the land.

I have a sound.
I build history.

One hundred thousand
fingers that find.
Call me Floyd.
I am here to purify.

My God, My Government

Christ said no more water,
and yet water.

The government said no crime
and yet, the water thieves.

Where have they taken my sheets,
my sketches, my loose beads?

In what corner of what dump
do they rot, open to the sun?

That star, it does nothing.
It claims no say over rain.

I cannot count all the lies
on two hands. The Good Book

misleads. We go back to the first
Earth. Darkness and deep ocean.

My county parson, believe me,
I am baptized the same

as these gone children,
mouths stuffed with rivers into wine.

My Good Christ

what did I do   to bring water
was it my   birth

crime

You consume all   Your children
for a sin   unnamed

It's No Longer a Secret

What happens when the mute brook
—gold—is never plucked? It swells.

It cracks. Its meat—pale, scavenged
for the broken skin, the juice

of it. Do birds even turn
their eyes to it? Does the gilt

ruin without touch, without
a good man's teeth in it?

Floyd Spreads Famine on His Black Horse

". . . I looked, and behold, a black horse. . . ." —Revelation 6:5

He flashes his scale, my village besieged.
I prayed my prayers, but Floyd breaks
the bed where I first met Christ.

The minister houses my family. I rest beneath
his daughter's sheets. She sings hymns
in the morning, hymns at night.

Floyd, allow me to fatten your stallion
with all my sin. In this chamber,
my shadow I leave behind.

Cope, Children

Nature had run its course.
My whole house was underwater.
I saw the caskets float by.
My dog—dead. I felt everything.

We entered 2 x 2, confined in plain white
modular rooms, exposed by the trauma
to hope and medicine.
This forced relationship to questions.

Six Crows

I was dead for years—then the water
awakened me. Hurricane-choked, I swam

out of bed on my way to Jesus. Thirsting,
I fell through to a hacked land.

Around me—glint of bent glass.
Disappearing so quick after that first

taste, it's true, I was made for this.
Out in the fields—crows turn over

the land, dig holes to hide the useless
secrets I've kept with them.

Father Fills the Tanks with Bleach

I will be so clean living in our one large room
above the skeleton wood. A gutted excavation
where air tongues naked beams beneath.

Here, the water did not reach.
We stretch into dishonest dreams,
the breeze retaining the cuff of disease.

Behind curtains strung from the ceiling,
brother and I learn a new dark.
Mother tosses in her makeshift marriage bed.

And in the morning, I bathe in water unfit for touch.
Baptized in tarnish, washed in Tar River's ruts,
I greet the day with skin reeking of stain.

I climb down stripped stairs
into the gutted womb of our blessed home.

Homemaker

Floyd licks a dish clean.
Dark becomes dust. Somewhere,

all my daughters in the raven's throat.
These hands are wild things. These sounds

throttle each distant sheet, unmade.
Everything's watching now,

except the light and the tomorrow.
I've made a village out of lies—all mine.

Emzara Says

Look how lonely the world after rain.
I lie outside the lions' cage, wander

through halls of sparrows—their hymns
cluttered with each dog's whimper.

Noah, days are long without land.
I talk to the elephant. I tell her

this marriage was a mistake.
Maybe I was not meant to survive.

If you must keep me, keep me
from the ark's lip. Fish sing my name.

Dove, Twice Released

Emzara named me before
I last took flight. I sing the sound

on my little land, over
and over, calling me to myself.

I regret the olive branch.
I regret ever going back.

Once, I was untamed.
Forgive her, Lord.

Emzara cannot know
the burden of a name.

Two Decades after the Flood the Doctors Still Don't Know What Is Wrong with My Brother's Body

A pinprick of black—
he tells me he will never get
back that sliver of sight.

The thing is slow erosion.
Motor skills, it takes.
Swells the tongue.

What to call a ghost
of the body. Do you name
it, like a pet?

Unspecified in water,
in my brother wading.
One day maybe I will forgive

everything, but for now.

In My Mother's Land

Scorpions hide
among bent poppies.

In my mother's land is a plot
to bury me in.

In her land, the wind is a cannibal.
Gunmen aim a little off.

A father has fists and a red-letter bible.
Coyotes outnumber dogs.

Tomorrow she'll bury her mother.
I am mountains away, dreaming beneath

a horse on the wall without a name.
It cannot hear me when I'm bent in prayer.

It cannot see me when I hunger.
It has never finished a race.

My grandmother's city will burn.
The fire will spare each empty lot,

basements with the dead. The fire will spare
her home near the pond where baby mice rest.

I have felt little in the way of grief.
I am unpracticed at death

and do not ask to learn it.
Evening, and none of these roads look right.

All the while a storm mistranslating sky.
You know what all my sleeping mothers tell

me when they haunt like want?
I am enough—in my bed of sawdust.

I am enough—cultivated in a dawn of sherbet.
Woman. Forest-finished. Wild crest. A type

of scorched, the Goddess fleshed.

I Have Nothing More to Say on the Matter

The water took and the water takes.
It's lovely to be wanted, they say.

But the thing that wants is
without a proper mind.

Clouds smile down like madmen.
The ground tries to speak,

desperately tired as a moon.
I refuse another drop of rain.

Everything, even yesterday, stalks each
sleeper, tick tock dreaming the war away.

Notes

"When the Lady of the Lake Comes to Stay"

    The epigraph quotes Seattle-based editor Mavis Amundson.
    Source: Amundson, Mavis. *The Lady of the Lake.* Western
    Gull Pub., 2000.

"'1940, afternoon of July 6—'"

    This is a found poem.
    Source: Salmonson, Jessica Amanda. *Phantom Waters.*
    Sasquatch Books, 1995.

"'It's a damn strange lake.'"

    This is an erasure poem.
    Source: Salmonson, Jessica Amanda. *Phantom Waters.*
    Sasquatch Books, 1995.

"Mother, I Have Stolen Your Tongue"

    This is an erasure poem.
    Source: Meador, Betty De Shong. *Princess, Priestess,*
    Poet: The Sumerian Temple Hymns of Enheduanna.
    University of Texas Press, 2010.

"Floyd Spreads Famine on His Black Horse"

    The epigraph quotes the English Standard Version Bible.
    Source: "Revelation." *The ESV® Bible,* Good News
    Publishers, 2001.

"Cope, Children"

This is an erasure poem. Source: Russoniello, Carmen & Skalko, Thomas & O'Brien, Kevin & A McGhee, Susan & Bingham-Alexander, Dana & Beatley, Jennifer. "Childhood Posttraumatic Stress Disorder and Efforts to Cope After Hurricane Floyd." Washington, D.C.: Behavioral Medicine, 28. 61–71, 2000.

"Emzara Says" and "Dove, Twice Released"

According to the *Book of Jubilees,* Emzara was Noah's wife.

Section quotes came from the following sources:

Meador, Betty De Shong. *Princess, Priestess, Poet: The Sumerian Temple Hymns of Enheduanna.* University of Texas Press, 2010.

Thorp, Alice. "Introduction." *Flooded: Reflections of Hurricane Floyd.* Chapel Hill Press, Inc., 2004.

For the poems in "The Missing Ones," I relied heavily on the research in Dan Pontbriand's book *The Missing Ones,* which he published in 2014.

About the Author

Lauren Davis is the author of *Home Beneath the Church* (Fernwood Press) and two chapbooks. She holds an MFA from the Bennington College Writing Seminars, and she is a former Editor in Residence at *The Puritan*'s *Town Crier*. Davis is the winner of the *Landing Zone Magazine*'s Flash Fiction Contest and the *House Journal* Fiction Contest. Her work has appeared in numerous literary publications and anthologies including *Prairie Schooner, Spillway, Poet Lore, Ibbetson Street,* and *Ninth Letter.* Davis lives on the Olympic Peninsula in a Victorian seaport community.

www.ingramcontent.com/pod-product-compliance
Lightning Source LLC
Chambersburg PA
CBHW030856090426

42737CB00009B/1252